**FOCUS**
Reading for Success

# You and Me

**PROGRAM AUTHORS**
Richard L. Allington
Ronald L. Cramer
Patricia M. Cunningham
G. Yvonne Pérez
Constance Frazier Robinson
Robert J. Tierney

**PROGRAM CONSULTANTS**
Bernadine J. Bolden
Ann Hall
Sylvia M. Lee
Dolores Perez
Jo Ann Wong

**CRITIC READERS**
Maria P. Barela
Phinnize J. Brown
Jean C. Carter
Nancy Peterson
Nancy Welsh
Kay Williams

**SCOTT, FORESMAN AND COMPANY**
Editorial Offices: Glenview, Illinois

Regional Offices: Sunnyvale, California •
Tucker, Georgia • Glenview, Illinois •
Oakland, New Jersey • Dallas, Texas

ACKNOWLEDGMENTS

Text
Adaptation of "Take One Apple" from EATS by Arnold Adoff.
Copyright © 1979 by Arnold Adoff. By permission of Lothrop,
Lee & Shepard Books (A Division of William Morrow &
Company) and Curtis Brown, Ltd.

Artists
Charles, Don: Page 63; Eberbach, Andrea: Pages 42–43;
Frederick, Larry: Pages 22–23; Halverson, Lydia: Pages 6–20;
Kock, Carl: Pages 30–35; Magnuson, Diana: Pages 24–29;
Miyake, Yoshi: Pages 50–55; Nicklaus, Carole: Pages 44–49;
Patterson, Diane: Pages 38–41; Sanfilippo, Margaret: Pages 21, 63

Photography
Roessler, Ryan: Pages 36–37, 56–61

Cover Artist
Marla Frazee

ISBN 0-673-72650-9

1991 printing
Copyright © 1988, 1985

Scott, Foresman and Company, A Division of Harper Collins *Publishers*.
Glenview, Illinois. All Rights Reserved. Printed in the United States of
America.

# Contents

Stories by:
Liane Beth Onish
Sallie Runck
Mary McCarroll White

# You and Me

# Who is Red Ridinghood?

# Red Ridinghood

Red Ridinghood wants to see Grandma.

 I can put apples into my  .

I can put big red apples into

my  for Grandma.

 I will walk to see Grandma.

I like to hear the red  bird .

Grandma likes to hear the bird .

Grandma will come out to hear

the red bird .

 Hello, Red Ridinghood, hello.

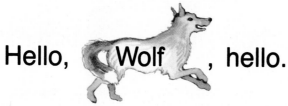 Hello, Wolf, hello.

I have red apples.

I have big red apples for Grandma.

I put the apples into my  basket .

Red Ridinghood will walk to see Grandma.

I will not walk.

I will run to see Grandma.

 Hello, Grandma, hello!

Grandma jumps up.

Grandma runs out.

The wolf walks into the house.

 Hello, Grandma, hello.

I put apples into my  basket .

Come out to eat and play.

Come out to hear the  bird .

Get up, Grandma, get up!

# Will Red Ridinghood See Grandma?

 Hello, Red Ridinghood, hello.

Walk into the house.

I can not get up to see you.

I can not get up to play.

Red Ridinghood walks into the house.

 Grandma, you have big eyes !

 I can see you with my big eyes !

 Grandma, you have big  ears !

I can hear you with my big ears !

 Grandma, you have big teeth !

 I can eat you with my big teeth !

 The wolf !

Red Ridinghood jumps up.

Red Ridinghood runs out.

The  wolf runs out.

 I hear Red Ridinghood!

I hear a wolf !

The  wolf wants to get

Red Ridinghood.

The wolf will not get

Red Ridinghood.

I will make the wolf run.

Woodcutter makes the wolf run.

 I like you, Woodcutter.

Come have some apples.

I put red apples into my  basket .

I put big red apples into

my  basket .

*To be read by the teacher*

# Take One Apple

## by Arnold Adoff

Take one apple,
wash and dry and
eat it up and down
and sideways to the core,
then take one apple more.

# Using Things

# Bubbles in the Room

 Who wants to play?

Who can run to the table?

Who can keep the

bubbles in the pan?

A girl ran with the pan.

The girl ran to the table.

 I have bubbles in my pan!

I ran with the bubbles !

A boy ran with the pan.

The boy ran to the table.

 I have bubbles in my pan.

I ran with the bubbles !

Tim ran with the pan.

The  puppy ran into the room.

The puppy ran to the table.

Tim saw the puppy jump up.

Do not jump up!

Tim saw the pan fly to the table.

Tim saw  bubbles fly to the table.

Tim saw bubbles fly in the room.

No, no!

I have no  bubbles in my pan.

But I do have bubbles in the room.

I have no cake to eat.

But I do have a funny puppy.

# The Happy Pan

 I will make a cake in the pan.

 But cake is not good for a happy pan.

I want a 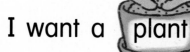 plant .

The pan ran to get a  plant .

A mouse saw the pan.

The mouse put the pan into the lake.

 I like boats.

The pan is a good boat.

 But I want to get a  plant .

The pan ran to get a  plant .

A bear saw the pan.

The bear ran with the pan.

 I like kites.

A pan is a good kite.

 But I want to get a  plant .

The pan ran to get a  plant .

The pan ran to a house.

The pan saw a girl in a room.

The pan saw a  plant in the room.

 I like the  plant !

I do, I do!

 Do you want a happy pan?

Do you want a happy pan for

the  plant ?

The girl put the plant into the

happy pan.

 The boy has no cake pan.

The mouse has no boat.

The bear has no kite.

But I have a  plant

A  plant is good for a happy pan!

# Just for You

1.

2.

3.

4.

5.

# Hello, Little  Kitten

# Helping Out

# Barb Likes Pizza

Barb said, "Hello, Grandma."

Grandma said, "Hello, Barb.

I put some pizza out on

the table for you."

Barb saw a hat, but no pizza.

Barb said, "I have to talk to you!

I can not find my pizza."

Grandma said, "I put it out

on a table.

I will go out to find the pizza."

Grandma and Barb ran out the door.

John ran to the door.

Grandma said, "You talk to John.

I will go find your pizza."

Barb said, "Hello, John.

Grandma put my pizza on a table.

But Grandma and I can not find

the pizza.

Can you find it?"

John said, "Yes, I can find it."

John said, "Your pizza is on the table."

Barb said, "I see a hat on the table.

But I do not see the pizza."

Grandma said, "I can find it.

The hat is on your pizza!

Who put the hat on your pizza?"

John said, "I put the hat on it.

I saw a fly on the table.

Do you want a fly to

eat the pizza?"

Grandma said, "No, no, the

pizza is for Barb!"

# Mom Gets a Cake

Al ran to talk to Dad.

Al ran to the door.

Al said, "I can bake a cake for Mom."

Dad said, "I will bake it with you.

But Sue has my red pan."

Al ran to talk to Sue.

Al ran to the door.

Al said, "I want to bake a cake.

Do you have the red pan?"

Sue said, "Yes.

But I have paints in it."

Al ran to talk to Dad.

Al said, "Sue has paints in
your red pan."

Dad said, "I have a tan pan.

I can bake in it.

Yes, I can bake little cakes.

I will bake little cakes for you."

Dad said, "You go out to play.

The cakes will bake."

Al ran out the door.

Al ran in to talk to Dad.

Al saw the little cakes.

Dad said, "I can bake little cakes.

Can you make a big cake for Mom?"

Al said, "Yes, I can!

I can make a big cake for Mom."

Al said, "Do you like the cake?"

Dad said, "Yes, I do like it!

Mom will like your cake!

Go to the door.

Give Mom the cake!"

# A Book for Dan

Reading
Bonus

Mr. Green put a book on the table.

Mr. Green said, "I have a book.

It is a good book to read.

You will like it."

Dan said, "I want to take the

book to my house.

I want my mom to see the book."

Mr. Green said, "Take it.

But do not keep it for long."

Dan said, "My mom will like

the book!"

A girl said, "No.

Your mom will not like it.

Your mom will like my book!"

A boy said, "Your mom will not

like your book, Dan.

No, your mom will like my book!"

Dan saw Mom.

Mom said, "Hello, Mr. Green.

I have to take Dan."

Dan said, "Mom, see my book!

See who is on the book!"

Mom saw the book.

Mom said, "I like the book!"

Dan said, "See!

My mom likes it.

Mom and I will read the book."

*To be read by the teacher*

# I Want to Read

by Laurie Michaels

I want to read a
book with you.
I like the book and
you will too.
Come read and laugh
the time away.
A book can fill
a quiet day.

# Books to Read

## A Beach Day
by Douglas Florian

Where can we go on a hot
summer day? To the beach!
This book will make you feel
happy and cool.

## Where Is Clifford?
by Norman Bridwell

Emily Elizabeth has lost her big
red dog, Clifford. Where, oh
where, can he be? You can help
find Clifford. Look in this book.

The words below are listed by unit. Following each word is the page of first appearance of the word.

# Word List

## Unit 1, 6-21

Grandma 8

put 8

walk 9

hear 9

out 9

hello 10

have 10

up 12

get 13

## Unit 2, 22-41

room 24

table 24

pan 24

ran 25

saw 27

do 27

no 28

but 29

happy 30

## Unit 3, 42-62

pizza 44

said 44

on 44

talk 45

find 45

it 45

door 46

your 46

yes 47

Mom 50

Dad 50

bake 50

tan 52

Dan 56

take 57